A Note to Parents and Teachers

DK READERS is a compelling reading programme for children, designed in conjunction with leading literacy experts, including ... Moon M.Ed., Honorary Fellow of the University of Rea... ...iff Moon has spent many years as a teacher and teache... ...ucator specializing in reading and has written more than 1... ...ks ...or children and teachers. He reviews regularly for tea... ...journals.

Bea... ...l illustrations and superb full-colour photographs combine with engaging, easy-to-read stories to offer a fresh approach to each subject in the series. Each DK READER is guaran... ...to capture a child's interest while developing his or her ... skills, general knowledge, and love of reading.

The ... levels of DK READERS are aimed at different readin... ...es, enabling you to choose the books that are ex... ...ght for your child:

Pre-le... 1: Learning to read
Level 1: Beg... ...ing to read
Level ... ...ginning to read alone
Level ... ...ading alone
Level ... ...ient readers

The ... age at which a child begins ... can be anywhere from three t... ...ars old, so these levels are only a general guideline.

No matter which level you select, you can be sure that you are helping your child ... read, then read to ...

D0432766

LONDON, NEW YORK, MUNICH,
MELBOURNE and DELHI

Series Editor Penny Smith
Art Editor Leah Germann
DTP Designer Almudena Díaz
Production Angela Graef
Picture Research Myriam Megharbi
Dinosaur Consultant Dougal Dixon

Reading Consultant
Cliff Moon, M.Ed.

Published in Great Britain by
Dorling Kindersley Limited
80 Strand, London WC2R ORL

8 10 9 7

A Penguin Company

A CIP record for this book is available
from the British Library

ISBN-13: 978-1-4053-1490-9

Colour reproduction by Colourscan, Singapore
Printed and bound in China by L Rex Printing Co., Ltd.

The publisher would like to thank the following for their kind permission
to reproduce their photographs:
a=above; c=centre; b=below; l=left; r=right; t=top; b/g=background

Alamy Images: Robert Harding Picture Library Ltd 20-21 b/g, 31cr b/g. **Corbis:** Matt
Brown 26-27 b/g; Larry Lee Photography 18-19 b/g, 30cl b/g; W. Wayne Lockwood, MD
4-5c b/g, 8-9 b/g; Charles Mauzy 5tcl b/g, 24-25 b/g; Craig Tuttle 4br b/g, 14-15 b/g,
16-17 b/g, 28-29 b/g, 31bcl b/g; Jim Zuckerman 6-7, 30cb b/g. **DK Images:**
Jon Hughes 4-5c, 8-9. **Getty Images:** J.P. Nacivet 22-23 b/g, 31tr b/g;
James Randklev 4c b/g, 10-11 b/g.

All other images © Dorling Kindersley
For more information see: www.dkimages.com

Discover more at
www.dk.com

DK READERS

Meet the Dinosaurs

DK

A Dorling Kindersley Book

Watch out!
Here come
the dinosaurs.

Here is the scary Tyrannosaurus (tie-RAN-oh-SORE-us). It has sharp teeth.

Tyrannosaurus

teeth

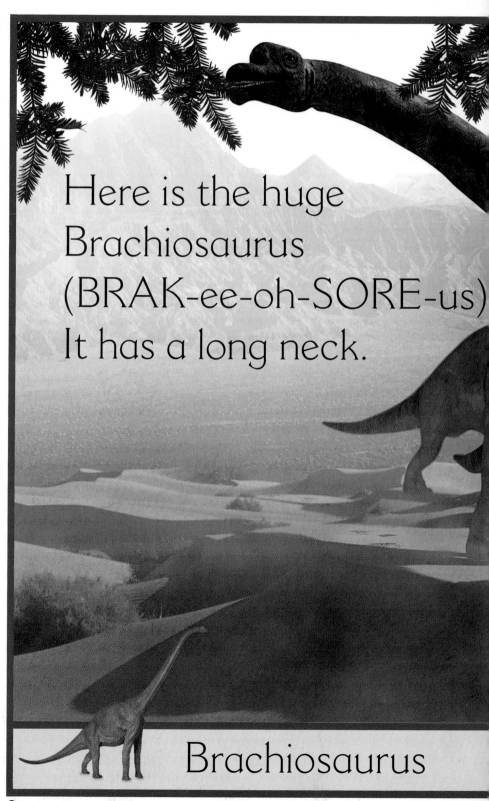

Here is the huge
Brachiosaurus
(BRAK-ee-oh-SORE-us)
It has a long neck.

Brachiosaurus

neck

Here is the tough
Triceratops
(try-SER-uh-tops).
It has three horns.

Triceratops

horn

Here is the fierce
Velociraptor
(vell-OSS-ee-rap-tor).
It has sharp claws.

Velociraptor

claw

crest

Corythosaurus

Here is the noisy
Corythosaurus
(koe-rith-oh-SORE-us).
It has a bright crest.

Here is the small Compsognathus (komp-sog-NATH-us). It runs quickly.

foot

Compsognathus

Here is the clever
Troodon
(TROE-oh-don).
It has large eyes.

Troodon

eye

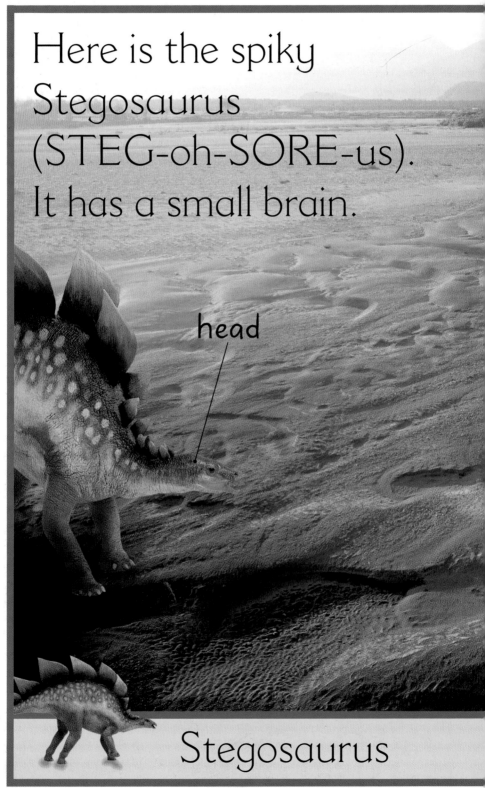

Here is the spiky
Stegosaurus
(STEG-oh-SORE-us).
It has a small brain.

head

Stegosaurus

Here is the bird-like
Gallimimus
(gal-lee-MEEM-us).
It has slim legs
and a beak.

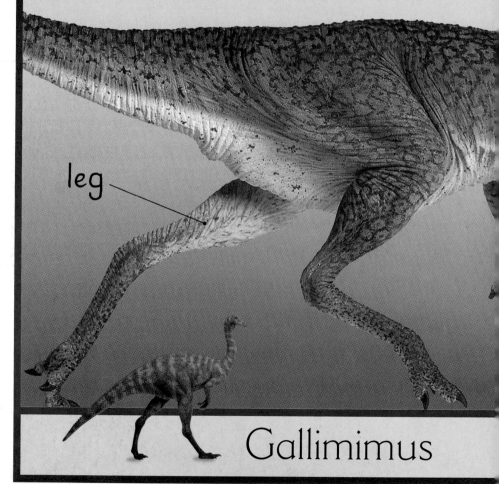

leg

Gallimimus

beak

spike

Iguanodon

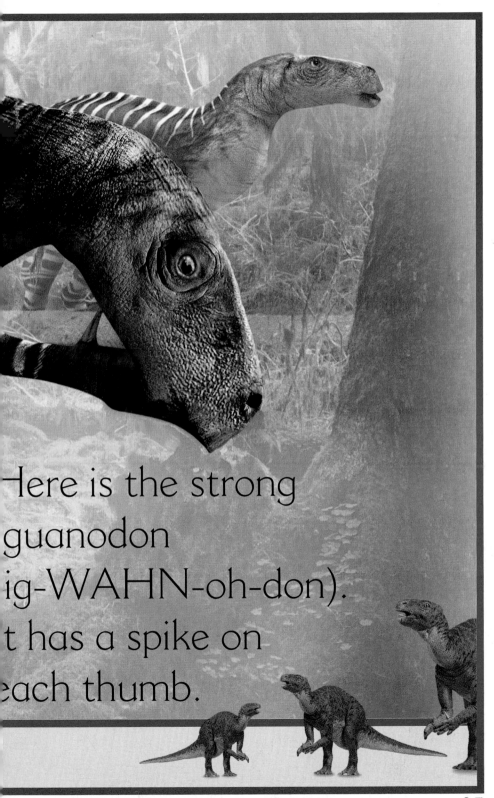

Here is the strong
guanodon
(ig-WAHN-oh-don).
It has a spike on
each thumb.

Here is the plant-eating
Stegoceras
(STEG-oh-SER-us).
It has a thick skull.

skull

Stegoceras

Here is the armour-plated Ankylosaurus (an-KIE-luh-SORE-us). It has a tail club.

Ankylosaurus

club

Which dinosaur do you like best? The one who is...

clever?

scary?

bird-like?

spiky?

noisy?

Picture word list

Tyrannosaurus
page 6

Brachiosaurus
page 8

Triceratops
page 10

Velociraptor
page 12

Corythosaurus
page 14

Compsognathus
page 16

Troodon
page 18

Stegosaurus
page 20

Gallimimus
page 22

Iguanodon
page 24

Stegoceras
page 26

Ankylosaurus
page 28